Above: New Apprentice Seaman at Sheephead Bay
Merchant Marine Training School in New York

Below: Able Seamen on shore Leave in San Francisco and Partying

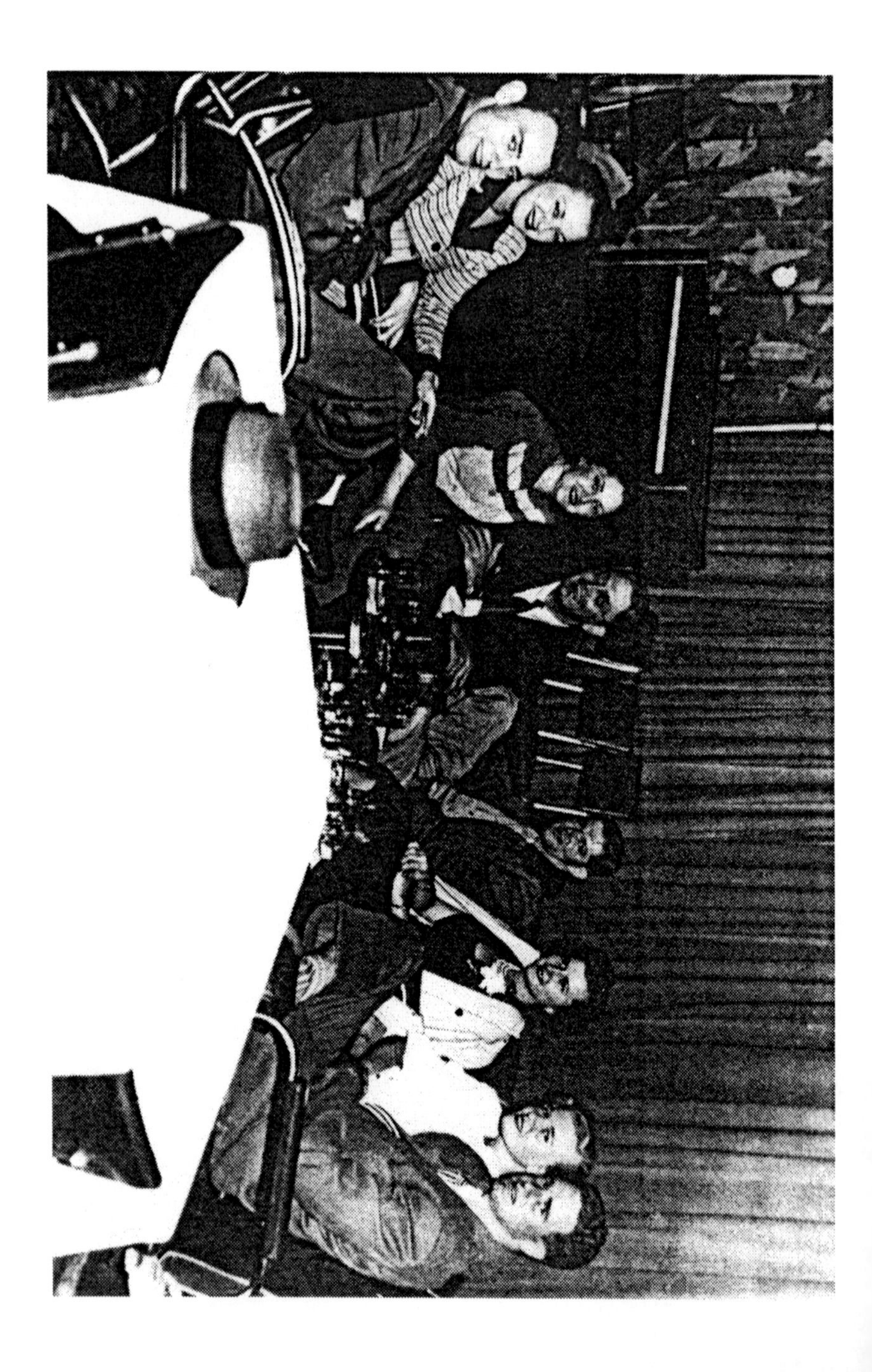

Note for Librarians: A cataloguing record for this book is available from Library and Archives Canada at www.collectionscanada.ca/amicus/index-e.html
ISBN 1-4120-9218-3

Printed on paper with minimum 30% recycled fibre.
Trafford's print shop runs on "green energy" from solar, wind and other environmentally-friendly power sources.

TRAFFORD
PUBLISHING™
Offices in Canada, USA, Ireland and UK

Book sales for North America and international:
Trafford Publishing, 6E–2333 Government St.,
Victoria, BC V8T 4P4 CANADA
phone 250 383 6864 (toll-free 1 888 232 4444)
fax 250 383 6804; email to orders@trafford.com
Book sales in Europe:
Trafford Publishing (UK) Limited, 9 Park End Street, 2nd Floor
Oxford, UK OX1 1HH UNITED KINGDOM
phone +44 (0)1865 722 113 (local rate 0845 230 9601)
facsimile +44 (0)1865 722 868; info.uk@trafford.com
Order online at:
trafford.com/06-0972

10 9 8 7 6 5 4 3

RISE AND FALL OF AMERICAN MERCHANT MARINE (NOT THE ROMAN EMPIRE)

by
Jack Forrest Harry

Jack Harry

ALL THROUGH MY life I'd wanted to appear older than I really was, seeing everyone as more mature and worldly when I entered first grade and thereafter during the years of the Great Depression, only because, as my father proclaimed, "the State says you have to go to school. We can't afford sending you. We can't afford . . . eating." thus instilling in me a lifelong sense of inferiority. Shaking his head, he watched my mother lead me off to that first day of school, unaware of the burden he'd placed on me, unaware also of how this feeling of worthlessness would drive me through life.

The Peter Principle states: man rises to his own level of incompetence. If self-worth, as my father instilled, had dictated my future I'd probably have become a ditch-digger at best. It didn't; instead, it drove me to do better, to cast off the chains of desperate poverty, and now, with the turn of the century close in front of me, I knew that by sheer will I had risen far above my level of incompetence, but I still did not feel sure of myself, believing I should seem younger than my 70 years to even think of succeeding in this one final accomplishment pending.

Standing before the imposing edifice representing Washington's Labor Department, the honking of autos and clipped pieces of conversation from pedestrians on Constitution Avenue were lost as I contemplated the importance of what lay before me. From that day long ago when my father made me feel worthless, I hadn't moved mountains but had done something challenging. I had sailed to all corners of the world, risen to the top of my profession by obtaining a Ship's Master's License. If that were not enough, I'd just been instrumental in forcing the two most powerful Maritime Unions in the nation into a court ordered election with me as a Presidential Candidate.

Even though this seemed monumental, I knew it might only be a Pyrrhic Victory. Sadly, the U.S. Merchant Marine faced extinction. If I were to win this contest to become President of this merger between the Masters, Mates and the Marine Engineers associations, it was entirely possible I might preside over the demise of the entire U.S. Merchant Marine. It was a very sobering thought, especially for me who 50 years before who'd seen the fleet in all its glory represented by thousands of ships which no other power could possibly emulate or challenge.

At that time. From there the U.S. flag merchant marine became an industry to set world standards, standards which no other nation even tried to emulate because of cost, which led to the S.S. United States, fastest passenger vessel ever designed, and other technological developments such as container ships and barge carriers. Of course foreign carriers with no interest in safety features required of U.S. carriers soon adopted all our designs with the result that foreign shipping grew while over time America became less and less a maritime power, its fleet dwindling to the next-to-nothing shell sailing today, unable to compete with foreigners who were unhampered by safety requirements but well subsidized by their flag nations who knew that carrying their commerce was an essential requirement for any pretender to world power.

The U.S., on the other hand, vocally supporting free world trade, progressively eliminated all forms of subsidy for its merchant marine, both in ship building and ship operations. Since the U.S. was from day one the major world market this meant that, as American shipping lines failed, more and more of its commerce was carried on foreign flag vessels. It was a sellout of major proportion which benefited more affluent American citizens at the expense of U.S. working people and security than anyone really knew because many of the foreign flag lines were often dummy companies for U.S. citizen owners. This was particularly true of flag-of-convenience companies, registered in Liberia or Panama, which plied routes in direct competition with U.S. shipping.

For a time most citizens did not worry much because we were in a life and death Cold War with the Soviet Union and our military surely knew best what to do. The Soviet merchant fleet was growing and provided its example of world power. But besides our own active fleet, despite its progressive reduction, we also had our mothballed fleet from the Second World War to back it up. And there was the flag-of-convenience fleet, which it's lobby loudly proclaimed, was an "effectively controlled" fleet of ships prepared to support any U.S. Military need. That the several "police actions" and wars that occurred in the last half century which the U.S. became embroiled in produced many holes in the "effectively-controlled-fleet" strategy, when some of those ships' crews refused to sail into war zones where the U.S. was engaged, was little noticed because so many shipyards were busy with military work, construction and conversion in competition with the Soviet menace.

Then, the Soviet menace was no more; we won the Cold War but learned nothing about sea power.

During each military confrontation, from Korea to the Gulf War, the American Merchant Marine expanded, seamen who lost seagoing jobs to peace and were forced to begin careers ashore were called back, as ships were again taken from boneyards to bolster the fleet. But each time it was discovered that the older, laid up ships did not really measure up. Should that have been a surprise? We had led the world in maritime development and produced better, bigger and

faster ships. The fact that this effort subsidized foreign fleets more than our own wasn't the critical factor; that we'd largely made our emergency fleet non-effective was.

Shortly after my first retirement, merely 30 years back, the Union sent me to a World War II Victory Ship pulled from Suison Bay north of San Francisco to make ready, load and sail to Vietnam. Shipyard workers swarmed over the rusting hulk which was scheduled to be ready to receive cargo in ten days. The crew were assigned piecemeal. The Chief Engineer boarded with me, and I immediately felt sorry for him when, after going to the Engine Room to look at the plant, he came back, threw up his arms and said, "forget ten days! Give me six weeks and . . . maybe."

As it turned out, six was was optimistic. After two months in the shipyard, the vessel, freshly painted, was towed to a loading berth with last minute engine repairs to be completed there before even a dock trial for the engine could be made, not to mention any thought of sea trials.

I had protested leaving the yard before the engines were even tested. My protest fell on deaf ears. I was told the war effort demanded we begin loading cargo needed desperately in Vietnam and assured by shipyard management that engine repairs would be properly completed on the loading berth. It wasn't my first experience with learning of the power moneyed interests held over good management decisions; of course I knew another Suison Bay mothballed vessel was scheduled into the yard which desperately needed our berth or it might lose the contract and we had already exceeded our original scheduled stay by some 50 days, causing a jam in the yard that could be relieved only by getting rid of us.

I had visions of loading a full cargo and then being towed like a barge without engines to Vietnam.

I needn't have worried. Powers in the Maritime Administration had already ascertained the vessel was beyond repair, and once removed from the shipyard she was not sailed but was again deactivated. While the Government legal staff prepared briefs against the shipyard for failing to deliver on a contract, the vessel was sold as scrap and the crew was all paid off.

An S.S. Neversail Again, no encouragement for me, and, more important, sad commentary on any future for the United States Merchant Marine.

Where it started, how, why, was only a guess. As a 17 year old shipped from Sheepshead Bay, New York, to San Francisco, California, and on to an Army Transport loading troops for a recently surrendered Japan occupation, I very soon demonstrated a reputation as a "fast learner."

The term "old salt" was very important among seamen.

"You're . . . coming aboard as . . . Able Seaman?" The Chief Mate of the U.S. Army Transport General Howell muttered, staring at the papers I presented to him. "Is this right?" he added, still looking at them.

"I . . . think so," I replied, standing before him in my dress blue Maritime Service Uniform, unaware I was a step ahead of myself. The San Francisco streets were filled with uniforms of all services. It didn't matter that once I boarded a ship I ws no longer a Maritime Service Trainee. Since I didn't have anything to wear except my uniforms and seagoing gear, dungarees, etc., issued by the Maritime Service, I didn't think twice about wearing it, just as it didn't dawn on me the Maritime Service driver made a mistake bringing me here.

The Mate, a Mr. Spano, it said on his door, smiled. "Guess it's okay, you'll . . . have to do." He handed me back the papers. "But, as soon as you can I suggest you go buy yourself some other clothes."

"Clothes?" I drew back. "What's wrong with . . . these?" I nodded down at my blue uniform.

He shrugged. "Nothing . . . if you're going to be a trainee all your life. Right now you've become a civilian employee of the Army Transportation Corps. We want you to wear blue dungarees, blue shirt, and a white hat aboard ship. We don't care what you wear ashore. But . . . that's up to you." He turned away, as if dismissing me.

"Uh . . . Sir . . . where do I go?"

When the Maritime Service deposited me at the ship's gangway with orders I'd had enough trouble finding the Chief Mate's office, coming here only because the watchman had instructed me to when I reached him at the top of the gangway after puffing up it with my duffle bag slung over my shoulder. He'd also saved me from further unnecessary effort by telling me to drop my bag there, he'd watch it for me, while he explained where the Mate's cabin was many stairs - ladders - as I was soon to learn they were called aboard ship - up the superstructure just below the Bridge.

The Mate turned, frowning, "You never been aboard a ship?" he muttered.

"Yes, Sir. The . . . training ship."

"That's right." He grinned. "You're no old salt . . . haven't got your feet wet, have you?"

"My . . . uh . . . feet wet?"

"Let me give you a word of advice, Anderson, he said, becoming serious-faced. "Don't tell anybody you haven't shipped . . . or about that training ship. It'll only make your life hell . . . until you live it down. And get out of that uniform as soon as you can. If you want to wear a uniform . . . go out and buy yourself what most seamen wear, when not wearing civvies . . . blue trouser, blue jacket, but not a jumper like you got on, and white shirt, with black tie and Chief's cap with no gold braid." As almost an after thought, he added. "And . . . report to the Boatswain." He said it like Bos'n which, I soon learned, was the way the title of the most important unlicensed officer aboard a ship was always pronounced. I also was soon to learn the Boatswain, or, Bos'n aboard many ships was more important than many licensed officers as well, particularly an old salt Bos'n beside some of the junior officers cranked out of the maritime academies in support of the war effort.

These young officers marched aboard usually still in the uniform of the academy, like me even if I wasn't an officer, and also usually went straight to the Captain, instead of the Chief Mate because no self-respecting gangway watchman would give any officer instructions except to jump over the side. If he did, nine times out of ten the officer would haughtily tell him to mind hs own business, he knew what was what, and then march right up to the Captain who would at once cut out his heart by thundering, "Don't bother me! Go see the damn Mate!

Even green Engineers often got caught in this confidence-shattering trap, going immediately to the Captain's Office instead of the Chief Engineer's one deck down. They suffered the most because they got it twice, once from the Master and again from the Chief, who was angry to learn they believed the Master had any control whatsoever over them. This separation of power aboard ship was reflected keenly in the maritime unions, if less so aboard Army Transports which employed Government Civil Service Seamen. But Mates were often referred to as "Swab-jockeys" by Engineers, who were in turn were called the "black gang" by Mates even on government vessels.

I went out on deck from the Mate's room through

an open door I spotted, pausing on emerging, because I was rather overwhelmed by what I saw: the splendor of San Francisco Harbor filled with ships spread out before me.

San Francisco port of embarkation-debarkation for the Army Transportation Corps was Fort Mason, but the General Howell was berthed at Pier 45 because Fort Mason wa full, I'd learn later. Pier 45 was directly next to the famed "Fisherman's Wharf" which I'd also learn about later. Off to my right I saw the Oakland-Bay Bridge stretching out to the Island of Yerba Buena, attached to Treasure Island, and almost directly facing me was Alcatraz, a prison it was reported no one had ever escaped from and lived to tell about it. Between Alcatraz and me and as far as my eye could see beyond were hundreds of ships of all shapes and sizes laying at anchor, or, in some cases, steaming toward unknown destinations.

My gasp, because of the sudden view, could not be restrained. A small town boy whose sense of inferiority had been ingrained by a childhood of poverty had, by way of Sheepshead Bay Maritime School, come to view the splendor of one of the most beautiful cities and Harbors in the world which was filled with the enormous maritime power generated by America, and such an awe-inspiring view for a moment made me feel even smaller and more inferior in the face of it.

But pride soon replaced my feeling of inferiority;

pride because of what the U.S. had accomplished by steaming such a fleet. It was possibly that moment in time that made me decide I too must accomplish much, to continue the maritime tradition my country had made possible for me. Certainly, it was a view which remained etched in my mind as certainly and clearly as a view a mountain-climber might have after he has struggled to the top; the difference, in this case, was that I was determined to overcome the struggles that still lay before me, because, as the view of hundreds of ships told me, anything, even my personal climb of such a mountain, was possible. It was there, a mountain before me, and it would not remain there long but I must climb it.

Overcoming my awe, I found my way back down to the gangway, where the watchman and my duffle bag awaited me. He explained to me where the forecastle was, the foc'sle as it was known, where I and all the unlicensed deck crew were berthed. The difference between licensed and unlicensed seamen quickly became clear to me, especially in regard to living quarters. The foc'sle, populated by six seamen three bunks high per small room might have been luxury to me, but having a room to yourself as a licensed officer, or, at the most, two to a room if space were at a premium, made obtaining a Coast Guard License as a Merchant Marine Officer an important step up that mountain of the future facing me.

First, however, the watchman told me, I should

find the Bos'n, who would assign me to a room. Again he told me to leave my bag with him and go back to the fantail at the stern or rear end of the ship where the deck storeroom was located where I'd probably find the Bos'n. If he was not there I should return to the gangway, and the watchman would call the bridge for an announcement to be made over the P.A. system (Public Address). Which, the Bos'n always hated.

Thus began my West Coast career at sea, and when it ended I learned quickly how fast the American Merchant Marine was sinking.

Many times I sailed to the Far East and up and down the West Coast, once from San Francisco with an Alaskan Pilot aboard and down to Panama, where we proceeded to drop the one forward anchor aboard when ordered from ashore and it went all the way down to the bottom in about 300 fathoms of water and was lost. Then , since I was off watch and considered the only seaman aboard the wartime LST who knew how to handle the after anchor, I was called out on Overtime to drop the after anchor once the Captain had maneuvered to shallower water.

Once, I took vacation and flew home when my Mother begged me to, because, as she said, my Father was losing another house which my Aunt and Uncle, on my Mother's side, had kindly bought for them on land contract. Since, my Father admitted, he could not pay, I took over the contract and

I thought it was a bargain for my Uncle to charge me only 5% interest, but my Father raged thereafter since he'd expected me to get the 4% he got but of course never paid.

Once, toward the end, when I was aboard one of the new P-2 Two Stackers the Army Transport had taken over, when in the Far East, I went into Inchon, S. Korea, before the North attacked and started the war, but we knew something was amiss because no shore leave was allowed.

But like always,the U.S. Government guessed wrong and when we got back to Fort Mason we were told to prepare the ship for lay-up. I was told by the Port Captain not to come back to the West after my vacation, that I'd probably have a far better chance of getting on if I went to the new command in the east since the new Defense department was taking over and giving all the ships to the Navy.

So I flew home again, with little hope for the future, and this time my Father had a new problem for me. He seemed to blame my Mother for not shoveling coal ashes fast enough which was ridiculous, but I didn't argue with him when he recommended I put in a new oil fired furnace. He said it would be much easier on my Mother, and I agreed and did it. I managed to pay it off very fast, which certainly impressed him but I knew helped my mother more.

But when my leave was up I told my parents I was going to New York to ship out with no hope of getting a ship and time soon even though I had a letter of recommendation from the West Coast to the Command in the Brooklyn Army Base, BART, as it was known. The ships were still under Army command and not transferred by a new Defense Department, which would probably happen if I got a new ship and did.

But much to my surprise, I arrived at BART just when they were short of Able Seamen and I was quickly assigned to a C-4 troop ship sailing in one day and told to report aboard. Thus, began my career on the East Coast of a shrinking Merchant Marine.

While on the West Coast, and now on the East Coast, there had been such a thing as the Draft, which all seamen were subject to and deferred only when aboard ship for six months at a time. There had been what was known as the Draft Holiday, a short period of no draft until congress in 1948 enacted the Taft-Hartly Act and canceled the Holiday. So the Draft began all over again. It, again, became necessary for every seaman to seek deferment from the employer and stay aboard ship for long periods until he earned enough vacation, which was meager, to chance going ashore.

Since starting to sea women had always been ready and willing to share bar stools when sailors came into town on any ship; often providing more than just company, if asked. One time on the West Coast I lost my heart to a very nice young girl, much too young to be one of the usual; but she quickly tired of me and cast me aside. Since I was really smitten, it took me a very long time before I got over that.

But when I signed on to my first East Coast ship a very curious thing then occurred. The C-4 Trooper sailed the next day right on schedule, and empty, to begin what was for me my very first round the world sailing. Gossiping crew soon revealed that this ship, normally a C-4 Trooper, had been hired to sail to Naples, Italy and load Displaced Civilians and haul them through the Suez canal and down to Australia for discharge.

Of course gossip ran wild after learning that, but it quickly was choked off about any possible intermingling of willing passengers when the captain announced stringent new rules about fraternization between crew and passengers. Of course, many ignored the rules and usually got their just deserts. Often, but not always. Some romance was born and did thrive, especially when down in the intense heat of the Indian Ocean most clothing was cast aside revealing what everyone certainly wanted to see. Even ships officers began partying, almost openly, when some willing "stuff" as it was called then, came their way. It might have become a good time for all but it wasn't destined to last. The staff accompanying the passengers suddenly found reason to voice their disgust to the Captain and demand their rights.

And he knew it had got out of hand. He then announced the rules would be enforced and did so, having what became known as "Kangaroo Courts" held in his office and firing many at the next port of call.

Of course, it was many miles back to BART where any seamen could legally be sent ashore.

If this ended the open partying it did not end secret trysts. If any crew got caught in the act, as it was known, a full "Kangaroo Court" became his fate.

But when we reached Australia, expecting possibly mass exodus from the ship, it seemed curious that I had left the West Coast and went and shipped out on the East Coast to sail through the Suez Canal right back to the Pacific Ocean, even if the Southern Pacific Ocean was where Australia was located.

There were many willing and ready girls in New South Wales, Australia, where we docked. All the girls seemed ready to grab any "Yank" she could and often party with him in any way he wanted till dawn, which made for many missed watches and often fights ashore with Australian men, who disliked the Yanks all spreading around their money and grabbing all the good "birds" as the Australians already called them. The fact that the ship was only scheduled to stay two days there after the long trip down through the South Pacific, but due to the Longshoremen stopping work with any sign of a rain squall in sight, and there were many, stayed two weeks to unload the Cargo which the ship's crew certainly enjoyed when getting many more nights ashore to party with their new "birds" and drink more of the fabulous Australian Beer, the ship not only lost time but much crew as well. Shore jails tended to become filled, as did hospitals, which for some strange reason benefited me.

During the trip here I had been assigned to the 4 to 8 Watch. I had made it known I was studying for my Third Mates License, and my Watch Officer had been more than willing to help me with my studies. When on the West Coast I had gotten my Able Seaman's Certificate, on my second try after my good buddy friend had taken me to a bar and got me so drunk on beer the first try the Inspector told me I was too drunk to sit and to come back the next day sober, which I did and passed.

But when we lost so many crew members in Australia, the shortage of men created an opening on the Day Gang and the Bos'n offered me a job. I jumped for it, especially when he told me I'd be the number one painter aboard. What I didn't know was that he meant spray painter. By the time I learned it was too late. But I did become a pretty good spray painter, even if it turned out to be a very dirty job.

When we finally sailed from Australia, empty again, we didn't go straight back to the U.S. But had received orders to go to Java where the Dutch Troops who were occupiers fought and lost a war with the locals and were being thrown out but lacked transportation. So we were hired for a new mission to load the troops, their gear and sail them home to Holland. When we left Java, we were loaded much faster than we'd been unloaded in Australia, since the new Government wasn't interested in having defeated troops hanging around. Even if many girls in the barrooms were not happy with us or the Dutch Troops for leaving so soon.

But leave we did. This time through the Panama Canal, completing a round the world voyage only when we reached Amsterdam, Holland, unloaded our cargo and Passengers. Steaming through the canals to Amsterdam seemed special to many staring at the big ship passing them in their fields but the windmills were not concerned.

When leave was granted there were many more willing girls awaiting us in the many bars. We seamen realized it was a tradition. Girls waiting for new eager seamen to spend money for good times and much beer, like always. Before we sailed, I bought a souvenir - wooden shoes - to mail home to my parents and then thought nothing more of them until my mother wrote me that they were stamped on the bottom: MADE IN THE U.S.A..

The made in the U.S.A. Slogan changed over time as more foreign nations recovered. But the U.S. Merchant Marine being full of marketable ships led the way. Many Corporations, even many Americans set up in foreign lands and knowing good bargains when they saw them, bought up much of the massive fleet for pennies.

When we sailed from Amsterdam and back to

BART terminal completing the voyage, mass exodus from the ship ensued, many of it being the firings. I hadn't gotten caught or stood trial, not because I didn't refuse the many willing babes during the long voyage, but mainly because I was careful and also because the Bos'n and the Captain seemed to like me and the good paint jobs I was doing for them. They wanted the ship sparkling and I did my best to make it sparkle. So I stayed aboard. It also helped that it had become known I was studying for a license, which might become a raise in grade for me. Promotions were often frequent when crews paid off. It still hadn't become like it would be later with many men looking for work.

Once back in the Brooklyn Army Base, which was still Army even though the many M.S.T.S. ships coming there had been transferred to the Navy. We had by message our ship was put on a regular schedule of sailing to Bremerhaven, Germany, the U.S. Army Port of Call. Sailing there with U.S. Troops aboard and on the way back to the U.S. with Displaced Persons passengers because the vessel was on hire to the U.N. Displaced Persons Administration. Troop ship conditions were not really suitable for passengers which the U.N. And D.P. big shots had protested many times but since they got such a good deal by paying for only one way routing and as long as the ship maintained her schedule they couldn't complain too much. But the scheduling often drew complaints, sometimes even for the crew. Keeping to a schedule, especially during winter storm weather on the North Atlantic was sometimes very difficult. Of course, the Navy always said the Captain was in full charge of his vessel and could change the schedule when he saw fit. However, when he did he had to have proper justification backing him up all the way against the many nay-sayers who from comfortable armchairs ashore suddenly sprang up to doubt any stormy seas out on the Ocean.

New York to Bremerhaven became our route. It kept the ships sailing under the U.S. Flag while many others were sold to bargain buyers. For many, the Reserve Fleet Anchorage in Suison Bay on the West Coast and the James River on the East Coast became anchorage's from which the ships were often taken out but never kept sailing for long. So these anchorage's became known as the "Rust Bucket Fleets of the U.S.".

The girls of Bremerhaven were all ripe and willing to service seamen and there were also many women in the bars in New York. I even made friends with a beautiful blonde girl from the U.K. who served as a concubine on call for an American Diplomat when he was home from his assignment as Consul to Argentina or elsewhere.

But these trysts on each end of each voyage became very boring after a time. Only the imported British Blonde seemed worthwhile, even if she only wished to thrill me when she was free from her money-man. And then would only play with me in expensive bars or restaurants. She would never provide me with anything I really wanted because as she said when finally breaking it off she wasn't going to become another of my Bremerhaven girl friends. She had better quality already in hand, even if a bit older than both of us. When we split, it was a major blow to me because she was blonde and just as beautiful as the one who'd disappointed me so much on the West Coast years before. Now, it had happened to me on the East Coast with the same result.

But one voyage when we came into New York a package from my Mother came which when I opened it I did not like the letter it contained. Since the war in the Far East, the Police action, as I had characterized, had heated up. The North Korean Forces had overrun the South rapidly, pushing the allied Armies all the way down to the South. The Allied Armies had finally halted them by setting up what became known as the Pusan Perimeter. My package from home contained a letter from ny Draft Board ordering me to report for my induction physical exam.

I had put in for leave from the ship to go to school to attend classes in studying for my Third Mate's license, and was stunned by the development. When I went ashore to my employer he told me if I wanted I could make arrangements to have my Physical in New York. I could attend classes and warn the instructor I might be absent for a one day physical exam. Which I did. There was no problem scheduling arrangements because the exam building was very near the Seaman's Church Institute where the upgrade classes were held. So it worked out very well for me, although the idea of having a pre-induction exam was worrisome. It seemed to mean the Draft Board did have me in their sights. But I was even able to occasionally see my blonde girlfriend whom I was still seeing. When I took my Third Mate's Exam at the U.S. Coast Guard, and passed it I'd always remember her saying to cheer me up before I went for my date with the Draft Board, "You can't ever keep a good man down!"

It was nice of her when were out one night, even if she was only costing me money to entertain her and not giving me anything I really wanted in return.

The next thing was that my ship returned from a voyage and I returned to her as an Able Seaman with a new Third Mate's License in my pocket. The Captain and others congratulated me. I was happy to be back on the ship with my employer's Deferment from the draft secure for another voyage at least.

Then, a Jr. Third Mate got into a fight in Bremerhaven and got beaten to a pulp by one of our own troops and was put into a hospital. The Captain promoted me to Jr. Third Mate in his place. It was nice to receive the promotion and increase in salary, but it wasn't the way I wished to move up, even if it benefited the Captain to have me available. But he did want me to get a new Draft Deferment and see about joining the Naval Reserve as soon as we returned to Brooklyn.

Then he was gone. A new captain came aboard and took his place.

In the mess of the change over I forgot all about the old Captain's warnings and didn't get a new deferment or join the Naval Reserve as all the other officers had done. And, when the ship returned from the next voyage my Mother sent me a new letter from the Draft Board, a new GREETINGS FROM THE PRESIDENT OF THE U.S.. I had passed my Physical EXAM and the BOARD had given me an induction date and ordered me to report and I had to leave the ship and return home. When I showed the order to my employer ashore, he only shook his head and said there was nothing he could do now. I'd have to go.

Which I did. I reported for Draft into the U.S. Army and hoped I would not be sent to Korea, where MacArthur had made an end run and in a blood bath invaded Inchon and began driving the North Koreans back up the Peninsula.

But the next 2 years which I had to serve in the U.S. Army were no bargain. I was first shipped to Fort Mead, Maryland, for indoctrination, and then down to Fort Eustis, Virginia, where I underwent first Basic Training, which seemed like Déjá Vu. I was going through Basic Training a 2nd time after having Boot Training before in Sheepshead Bay, New York, before they first shipped me out. Now it was the same thing again.

But then the army seemed to get smart. After Basic, instead of shipping me out to be a foot soldier, they sent me to a Harbor Craft Crewman's course, and intended to entice me into liking the Army. But I did accept their offer of promotion to PFC because when they shipped me north to sail a Landing Craft Unit around Goose Bay Labrador, I knew I'd made the right decision so I could leave the Army after my two year's active duty requirement. The fact that I had to serve 6 additional years in the Reserve did not interfere with my shipping back out when I was discharged as long as I reported for duty on a ship with MSTS within 30 days, which I, of course, did.

After taking several weeks leave to visit my Mother and Father, I went again to the Brooklyn Army Base to claim my Junior Third Mate's job which by law was supposed to be waiting for me. Everyone in the Office seemed happy to see me back, if not the Jr. Third Mate I was forced to bump off the new ship in port, another C-4 Trooper newly hired by the UN Agency on DPs to bring them back to the U.S. after running troops to Bremerhaven.

The girls in Bremerhaven were all ready and willing to party but my girl in New York was gone, having her money-man buying her a new house in Greenwich Village. She imported her own Mother to live in it with her when he was away on assignments.

After three trips back and forth over the North Atlantic even the Bremerhaven girls started to seem too much, too costly and too willing and eager to marry. They had all changed, and had staked out certain seamen for their own futures.

Then, on the fourth trip back to New York in the middle of the North Atlantic, I met the woman who would become my wife for the rest of the century. She was a very pretty passenger and after seeing her for a year between voyages we both took the plunge, as it was called. She miscarried once but together we had three children, two boys and one girl. They were all fine children. My wife was a great wife for a seaman following me from port to port and raising our children so they were a credit to us both . But when she decided to put down her anchor and stop following me from port to port she picked out the home she wanted to live in the rest of our lives and in no uncertain terms made me buy it for her. It was a major moment in a seaman's life. I still had to go to sea with what had now become the Military Sea Lift Command because a new Admiral had taken charge. He decided there could be no MSTS in the Navy since there could not be a service with a service like the Navy. Then Unions moved in when the President declared they could organize government services and the organizing was fair game for them all. It was legal to sign pledges with as many as one wanted. I chose the Masters Mates and Pilots and joined, realizing that it was the nearest to what I wished to sail, and also realizing in some small manner it might provide some security for my future.

I sat for my 2nd Mate's License while we lived together in an apartment in Bay Ridge, Brooklyn, N.Y. The apartment was very near the Army Terminal where most MSC Ships docked. After writing for 7 days I passed the exam and was given a new 2nd Mate's License. We moved back to my home state and she followed me with our first son. But trying to live together with my parents did not work out and we found our own place. Our second son was born in Connecticut and the next big occurrence happened when we had our daughter born in Virginia. Then my Father died and my wife decided to drop her anchor when she found the home she wanted.

The next major thing that happened was when I retired from the Military Sealift Command, early, with 27 years of service, counting the 2 years I had been forced to serve in the U.S. Army.

But this did not end my seagoing. Supporting a family and paying off a new home meant I had to continue sailing and so I went to the Master's Mate's and Pilot's Union Hall and was pleasantly surprised that I had guessed right again when I had maintained my membership, even though my wife often complained about paying dues to the Union while I was still in Government Service. My sudden retirement did surprise her but she never complained about receiving my retirement pay, even if it turned out not to be enough.

But when I told her about the Union, nightmating and being paid after working one night or many; and when I added I could ship out anytime and would be paid in full after signing off any vessel, plus receive immediate pay for vacation time earned, to be served when I could not register to ship out again, she didn't object. Thus began my career sailing commercial merchant ships and going to many ports worldwide.

Sometimes I hated it; sometimes not. But it took at least a week to get used to leaving even if the money was good. I didn't know how much my wife and family missed me. But I did know she was doing a fine job in caring for the family when I was gone, even though, each time I returned I seemed to have much work waiting for me to do which she always indicated was my job to do. I didn't object, because she never objected to my coming home and in a sense taking over from her and trying to relieve her of so much work. Even if she once in a while complained, she never became intense about it.

Once when I was home between voyages, I organized and scheduled a vacation for us all. It was the year ending the 2nd century of America when I loaded the family of 5 into the blue van I had bought and towing a tent camper behind began a tour of the whole of the United States. I knew that this would be the last time we would all be together and could afford to do it. Our oldest son would be starting college soon and the others were going to different schools and into different grades. Gasoline would no longer remain as cheap as it was then. So we would have to do it that year or forget about it forever.

So, off we went, our family of 5, covering 11,000 miles in six weeks around the country. We spent July 4th, 1976 up at the top of the Space Needle in Seattle, Washington, which was the real celebration of 200 years of U.S. History. We'd come from the east coast down to Stone Mountain near Atlanta, then to New Orleans, across southern U.S., all the way to Long Beach, California, where the Queen Mary was berthed as a tourists' attraction, then up the West Coast through San Francisco, which had already changed considerably from what I remembered as had Seattle, which I also remembered well.

Then we went across the upper U.S. returning to our old farm house, which my wife had wanted. I was continually fixing it up between voyages. It turned out that I actually spent more time and money fixing the house up than we had to pay when we bought it. But my wife wanted it and I was eager to make her happy because she was a fine mother of our children and a fine wife for a man who seemed to have to be at sea so much of the time.

The next thing I realized, after shipping with Sea Land on their new SL-7s which they had had built in Europe and which I always had to go to New York when my shipping card was old enough to catch. (Another definite indication of how the Merchant Marine was shrinking) . One trip when I came ashore to take my vacation I went to the U.S. Coast Guard and sat for my Master's License. I passed the Exam, which was actually easier than before because there was less writing. It mostly consisted of multiple choice questions, a new style the U.S. C. G. had instituted, and which made it possible to finish on their also instituted schedule. I had studied hard for it and when I passed it and was given my new MASTER'S LICENSE I figured I had finally achieved the end of my career by rising from a lowly Apprentice Seaman to MASTER of any steam or motor vessel of any gross tonnage sailing the seas, which were all becoming fewer and mostly foreign flagged.

But shipping out on U.S. ships had become so difficult it became necessary to register in any port and let your shipping card get very old, sometimes so old it expired and forced you to re-register. This made it very difficult to ship. If it got old enough one always had to go to another port like New York, where most vessels paid off to get any kind of shipping job. New contracts had been negotiated with the companies, which had dwindling vessels in their fleets, and they all insisted on assigning two permanent Masters to every vessel they had. Because as they maintained, they were paying them full pay for the full year and vacations had gone through the roof. There were many Unions on every ship and each union insisted on special rules and each insisted on JURISDICTION, a term which ultimately spelled the end of the U.S. Flag Merchant Marine.

But the next major event which happened to me came when I paid off a Sea Land SL-7. When I went into the Norfolk Port Hall to register, the Port Agent hired me to replace his elected assistant, who had died.

Thus began my first job ashore and it became hectic. First I had to drive every day to the Norfolk Union Hall and open it and this while I was on vacation paid per diem salary. Then as an APA, as it was called, I was expected to go aboard vessels coming into port. Even though the commercial ships coming in were fewer, many more military vessels did come in, particularly Military Sealift Command Vessels which I was really familiar with, and I soon became the East Coast Government Employees Representative of the Union.

But before I retired from the MSC, as it was called, something happened which any thinking person should have noticed was making the U.S. Merchant Service less than with any good future. In 1949, while the Merchant Marine was still viable, U.S. architect W. Gibbs began construction of the S.S. United States, the pride of the Merchant Marine. Which when completed in 1952 on her maiden voyage won the blue ribbon from the Queen Mary for the fastest crossing of the Atlantic Ocean. This record she would maintain as pride of the U.S. Lines Fleet until she was retired in 1969.

This retirement was a beginning of the end for the mighty U.S. Merchant Marine. But it wasn't the end, until under President Ronald Reagan the entire U.S. Lines declared bankruptcy and went belly up with it's entire fleet. It had been one of the largest in the world until then, which then made the U.S. a SECOND RATE Merchant Power.

At about the same time, the Master's Mate's and Pilot's Union and the Marine Engineers Beneficial Association were both at virtual war with each other over jurisdiction - the dreaded fights of unions. Both Unions decided to poll their members. Only the MM&P decided to conduct the poll legitimately but when it passed nothing thereafter happened. Thus, the other unions did not bother until it was too late to reverse the trend of the disappearing Merchant Marine.

When I went ashore to my first shore job and even though appointed I went through hectic times to survive, believing the Port Agent who had appointed me and the current MM&P President that the other union, like the Marine Engineers were all out to sabotage the MM&P and take away all our last shipping jobs, as many others also believed.

It was a very trying time. What companies that were left flying the U.S. Flag on their fleet ships decided to seek Union support to survive and agreed to establish a unified Washington Lobby, which itself became something of a larger firm than the Union it represented as only a few seemed to notice.

Finally, after traveling around the country, flying mostly, although not noticing that fewer ships meant more airplanes, and organizing the Army Corps, where I had started, then the Military Sealift Command, which was growing, then Navy Pilots, then negotiating new contracts for them all and supporting the current president of the union in his run against a newcomer who insisted on having the Union Divisions subject to proper accounting, and when the current president I had backed lost the election, I resigned and retired again, thinking that this was the end.

But, as small as the Merchant Marine had become, there was still room for more. The newly elected president, who was having problems of his own because most union officials who had lost set up to battle for their jobs, sought me out and said I had been right about the government workers I'd represented. He had not wanted me to resign, and asked me to come to work for him as a consultant. I almost laughed. But I did not laugh. The Port Agent who had hired me in the first place, but had himself lost the election, told me the new president deserved any support I could give him. I thought it over very carefully.

Thus, began my career as a Consultant for the dying Merchant Marine.

I had tried to get MM&P and MEBA to work more closely together, and in certain pass-through agreements between them they did start making attempts at cooperation. But for me, it seemed too little - too late. Cooperation was one thing - merging might have delayed the inevitable a little longer, but there seemed nothing on the horizon to save the dying American Merchant Marine. Jurisdiction between warring unions wanting to rule the industry continued to threaten the Union leg of the triangle supporting whatever was left of the mighty fleet which once sailed from U.S. Ports and now ruled mostly by foreign flags flying from Panama to China and elsewhere.

Speaking of Panama, one of the things I was called on as a consultant for the new president was to negotiate a new last contract between the Panama Canal Commission and the Pilots, both American and Panamanian, in Panama, before the Canal would be turned over to Panama by agreement between the U.S. Government and Panama at the turn of the century.

When it was agreed to meet in Panama I flew down and the meeting was held. Just as I had expected the Commission refused to accept our ground rules because they were interspersed with demands for an entirely new contract. So, we were forced to accept the Commission's ground rules, which were fair, but they were not willing to accept any points of negotiation until a first meeting, which was one basis for our filing an Unfair Labor Practice Charge.

As it turned out, Captain Ceely and I began working closely together and along with his assistant, Captain Jorge Teran and Peggy in support, we made up the Pilots negotiating team. Captain Teran was Panamanian and a good Pilot who'd been elected to office as Ceely's running mate and who was one of the lucky Panamanians who had graduated from Kings Point Maritime Academy in the U.S. And so received the 15% add on on his salary, which most Panamanian did not. He knew this gravy train would end when the commission was disbanded when Panama took over the canal by treaty, so he was planning to retire as Captain Ceely planned. Anyway, they made up a good negotiating team and Captain Ceely's idea of changing working rules and paying each pilot the same amount for any assignment went over big with the new Panamanian Pilots, but wasn't liked at all by the Americans, who believed this was the way to take away their 15% add on which it certainly would. It wasn't exactly liked by Captain Teran either.

So one could see what I was facing. To negotiate a new contact for so many pilots, each who had his own ax to grind, so to speak, meant I had to provide proposals that not only the Panama Canal Commission would accept but which the diverse group of Pilots I represented who all had individual wishes would also accept.

Which meant that I had to work closely with Captain Ceely and did. As I got to know him better, realizing how old I was getting, I began thinking of him as someone to relieve me once he retired, so I could fade out in time. I needed to fade away. I was getting very tired. Flying back and forth to Panama in between my many meeting with Navy and MSC and the Army Corps, many of them in Washington at their Headquarters and alternately at MITAGS. We all tried to abide by the Executive Order about partnershipping between Agencies of Government and Unions representing workers. Occasionally I had to fly to meeting such as to Houston, Texas, and then down to the Army Corps Dredge Wheeler when an Assistant Secretary of Army had scheduled a visit aboard. This was billed as his visit to announce the Administration had bowed to the political lobbying of the private dredging industry and intended to deactivate the Dredge Wheeler, which has the only only remaining Army Corps Dredge on the Gulf Coast. The privates believed they had more than enough dredges to do the Wheeler's dredging on the Gulf Coast, and I met with the Assistant Army Secretary and even convinced him that laying up the Wheeler was a very bad idea. I was later to see my speech for the Wheeler's retaining operations more than justified when the midwestern floods inundated the Mississippi River system, requiring dredging not only by the Wheeler and all the available privates, but having the Army

Corps needing to bring the one dredge on the east coast, the McFarland, down to dredge and also order one of the dredges from the west coast - the new Essayons. The Essayons was needed to help in dredging the Mississippi in order to keep it open to traffic on the river as well.

I particularly liked the fact that when the bean pushers in the Portland Army Corps District attempted to deny travel pay to the Dredge Employees on their time off that I was able to call Ms. Tina Street and get her verification as she had been at the original negotiations of the Travel Pay Provisions paying back deck officers for travel when off duty was valid and had been intended to provide for just such circumstances, which naturally meant all aboard when off duty got the same. This was another time when Tina Street, who had become a high up person as Assistant to the Commanding General, became a great person in her own right, to me if perhaps not to the bean pushers in Portland, whose predecessors had been largely responsible for our negotiating such a provision many years in the past. That I and the MM&P received credit for this became immediately clear when the Captain, after flying home on a Corps provided airplane ticket wrote me and told me to send many applications for MM&P membership because his whole crew wished to sign up., I sent him some and wrote back that only Licensed Deck Officers could sign up. But we appreciated the response and we also appreciated the Assistant to the Commanding General, Ms. Tina Street, for being very honest and supportive. Whether it went over with the General or not, it meant she would be cheered by those Army Corps people serving under her.

But flying down to Panama meant I was actually working all the time. Captain Ceely managed to get permission to provide Air Tickets from Miami International to Panama for my wife and me, and he set us up in houses of off duty Pilots who had flown home to the States. So with my wife in tow we drove from North Carolina to Miami leaving our car with friends when we flew out. We also went down one time when the FLRA General Council Mr. Joe Swerdzewski had to fly down himself to meet with the Commission and get them to expedite the Presidential Executive Order for partnershipping since the delay there had become a glaring example which the Administration then was against.

It was then that I discovered that an Unfair Labor Practice charge I had filed against the Commission for failing to negotiate in good faith wages, which they now claimed they were not required by law to negotiate, and I claimed otherwise. They had already made offers in the informal meeting, which they now denied, but General Council Swerdzewski said that is might be possible they might be required to negotiate as my UFL Charge had appeared on his desk and was under consideration. When I met him face to face I took the opportunity to mention that

Navy had already negotiated wages for the Pilots and he indicated then that he had knowledge of the case and knew of my hand in it.

But the struggle I had to be under, flying often and more than I wanted, seemed to be wearing me out, and even my wife saw that I was working far too hard for far less than I was really worth. I told her then about my idea of training Hank Ceely to relieve me, since we were working so close together and it seemed a perfect opportunity. Since it seemed to me, if he could deal with such an agency as the Panama Canal Commission for so long, he would have very little trouble when he retired in a couple of years to dealing with other Government Agencies. And I would smooth the way with the MM&P President to get him assigned so I could rest easy knowing my Government Employees had a knowledgeable Representative in place of me.

When the FLRA finally ruled on my UFL that most of my proposals were negotiable, especially wages, we believed we had won a big victory, but when we next met with the Commission Negotiators we found they had learned "stonewalling" was an art form. They agreed to negotiate our proposals and then rejected them each, proposing instead their own counters, including the very same wage raises they had offered in informal negotiations in Florida. Their attitude was that they had a package of only so much money and could not offer more. If we wished to apply it to any special interest, they might consider that. When we proved to them how much the commission earned by each vessel's transit of the canal, and the pilots were the largest contributors to each transit, they dismissed it as hogwash and restated their own top figure for wage negotiation, agreeing only to talk about how to apply it to pilot earnings.

It was a very trying time. Our position of equal pay for equal work was rejected as a giveaway of what U.S. Citizen Pilots deserved for agreeing to be in Panama, which Panamanians who already lived there did not, and since those Americans on the Commission also received the 15% add on, none wanted to see anyone trying to give it away, which the U.S. Government might decide nobody deserved, which wasn't far from the truth. Colonialism still was present even near the end of the 20th Century.

But Captain Ceely decided to take the pay figures and add them together which produced new overtime figures which in a strange way added to what Panamanian Pilots received, which reduced in a sense the impact of the 15% add on for American Pilots, which the Commission Negotiators accepted, and we did finally manage to negotiate a new contract and submit it to the membership for a vote.

But the Pilots, through a concerted effort at infiltration of the Commission Spies, managed to get the agreement voted down, which meant that we had to resume negotiations all over again and we had gotten the Commission to agree to some new work rules, which they definitely did not like.

Because, when back in the United States, I was constantly on the go, and recognized that as far as the U.S. Flag Merchant Marine was becoming a hollow shell of itself, and most U.S. Flag Ships that had not run away to foreign flags were now operated by the U.S. Government, either by MSC with civil service crews, or, contracted to shipping companies under lowball agreements for stationing around the world to be on call for any emergencies, as those in Desert Shield/Storm had been called on at the beginning of that hostility and had responded as needed, I was running around and wearing myself out. But when the re-negotiations of the Panama Canal Contract had a date set, I again had to fly down to Panama and be in the negotiations.

As it worked out we managed to negotiate a new contract and again we submitted it to the memberships for a vote, and we were fast running out of time. The end of the century was fast coming up when the Canal and Territories would be turned over to Panama. The Pilots new they had to have a contract in place to begin new negotiations with a new competitor. The pilots passed the new Agreement, the Commission Administrator signed it and the Secretary of Army approved it and it was put into place and I breathed a sigh of relief.

My wife and I did fly back to Panama one more time to attend what was billed by Captain Ceely as a victory party and a well deserved vacation for him and me. But neither Captain Ceely nor I were really satisfied with the Agreement we had negotiated although we both realized it had been the best we could achieve, considering the many different cliques of pilots, each with its own secret ax to grind. Nor did the Commission with the defiance of its negotiators against giving any Pilots anything more than it figured they deserved make any more effort by us warranted.

When the party was over I explained to Hank Ceely what I had in mind for him, since I knew he would be retiring very shortly and he seemed sincerely interested and also recognized how old and tired I had become.

So back in the U.S. I continued my efforts to represent the many Government Employee Members of MM&P and sought as well to get all the Unions together as a solid group, agreeing as a group with Government Agencies when what they proposed seemed worthwhile or beneficial to the Employees we represented. Opposing such moves when we did not like where they were leading. I really believed I was making some good progress and also could see light at the end of the tunnel for me. Since Hank Ceely could become my relief once he retired and I got an agreement with Captain Brown to hire him in place of me after I filled him in on how to work with Government employees and their unions. Not that he didn't already know much, since he had dealt with the Panama Canal Commission for so long, but Government Relations in the U.S. were somewhat different when away from the insidiousness of "Jurassic Park South" which was a good joke but obviously understandable when one met other men who were so secure in their beliefs they ruled the world. Although their little empire was soon to pass away when the Canal became ruled by Panama by treaty.

But the U.S. Merchant Marine on which the Masters, Mates and Pilots, and other maritime unions had built their business, had also become just that, a kind of business itself, each union half opposed to each other union. As much as I hoped to get them to work together most of them felt it was in their own interests as far as Government Agencies were concerned. Although, there remained certain competition between them even there, as the Government Agencies contracting out ships made certain they received every lowball bid of unions competing against each other, and most companies still in the American Merchant Marine were mere shadows of their previous selves. They had already sent most of their ships to foreign flags but they encouraged each union to lowball every other union in every bid.

And the Government also encouraged it, because the Government through the U.S. Navy had become ruler of the sea and was therefore the biggest ship owner under the U.S. Flag and didn't understand why Merchant Mariner wages seemed so high when their Admirals seemed underpaid, even though their many fringe benefits made such wages the least of their incomes.

But when Hank Ceely retired and moved to his home in Florida I brought him to the Captain who remained MM&P President, and he agreed to hire him to replace me after I broke him in. So I took him to various Government and Union Offices and introduced him to everyone as my relief, after I saw to his obtaining the International President's Signature on his own contract as my replacement.

Thus I bowed out from more than 50 years I had seen as the largest U.S. Flag Fleet in the world become at the Century's end a shadow of its former self because all three legs of the triangle which had built and supported it for so many years had been pulled from beneath it, each for the same reason, pure greed as shipping companies sought whatever meager profits available, the all powerful Government sought to reduce taxpayer costs to spend on its super Navy, and each Union Official sought to remain in high salaried office.

At the century's end, it wasn't the FALL OF THE ROMAN EMPIRE, but it was the fall of the U.S. Merchant Marine as I had known it.

My Wife and I first met in the middle of the Atlantic Ocean, when she was transported as a passenger on a ship I was a Third Mate on, which was then known as Third Officer and she not only became my wife but she was my best friend. When she finally put our anchors down firmly for the last time in North Carolina she was a great raiser of the family she provided for me a seaman, and she and the family are pictured on the back cover.

Ships in
Beginning of End
VERNMENT FLEET

ON LEFT: Randi Cizewski, MM&P & MEBA Government Employee Representative
ON RIGHT: A Master or Mate still Sailing

The End!

Lightning Source UK Ltd.
Milton Keynes UK
UKOW05f0622090813

215108UK00002B/108/A